AMERICA'S LONG, DARK ROAD
A Quick Guide to Racism in America

by Mike Betteridge

My name is Mike. I am a 60-year-old white male. I am a banquet cook and enjoy my job. I am not associated with any organization, or religious or political group.

My mom and dad taught me that no one is better than me, and that I am not better than anyone else. They said to treat other people as equals and to judge them for nothing except who they are. Martin Luther King, Jr. said it best: "Judge a man not by the color of his skin, but by the content of his character."

I'm a nerd. I enjoy learning about things and read a lot. I have been that way my whole life. I was not able to go to college because my family was not able to afford it.

I believe that words and facts matter. With the current spike in attention to violence against black people, racial injustice and the Black Lives Matter movement, I can no longer remain silent about the *real* history of racism. The fact is, black lives have *never* mattered throughout U.S. history.

I will use facts and current archaeological theory in the discussion. The significant thing about theories is that they can change. As new evidence is discovered, a theory can evolve to a greater truth or become a failed theory. I hope you will fact-check anything I say that you doubt is true. In fact, I encourage you to fact-check everything I say. Doing research and learning new things is enjoyable to me. You may discover the same thing.

Let's talk about race, starting at the very beginning, with who we are, where we came from and how we got here. 28 million years ago, the Ice Age started. As ice accumulated in the northern hemispheres, the world's oceans dropped to 200 to 400 feet. Between 28 million and 3.2 million years ago, the jungles in Africa got smaller and grassy plains developed between the jungles.

As primates went from jungle to jungle, they were easy prey for predators from the air, land and water. 3.2 million years ago, "Lucy," and her relatives, the first bi-ped humanoids that could stand up and see over the grasslands to spot predators, had a better chance of survival. For the next 3 million years or so, at least 50 to 100 varieties of humanoids developed, from Australopithecus to Homo habilis, and so on. Then, between 350, 000 and 250,000 years ago, a humanoid species developed called Homo sapiens – which is us.

As the population of Homo sapiens grew, they began migrating throughout Africa. Their bodies, face shapes and skin color changed as they adapted to their new environments. Around 70,000 B.C., the eruption of the Toba volcano caused a volcanic winter and poisonous air that devastated the population. By the time it was over, there were only about 1,000 pairs of Homo sapiens left to breed going forward. The survivors, mainly from East Africa, began again, increasing their population, migrating, and adapting, with genetic changes, to their new environments.

Around 60,000 to 30,000 years ago, Homo sapiens began migrating out of Africa, to what is now Europe, eastern Asia and Australia. Again, genetic changes occurred that helped them survive in their new environments. However, the migration into Europe and east Asian was different, because, for the first time, they came across another humanoid group, the Neanderthal.

When the species mixed, it created a hybrid sub-species of Homo sapiens. That left the African Homo sapiens as the only "true-blooded" Homo sapiens, because, after that, nearly all European and east Asian populations had Neanderthal DNA. If you don't believe me, get a DNA test.

In the Northern Hemisphere, around 10,000 to 8,000 years ago, the loss of pigmentation in Homo sapiens is noted, and "white" Homo sapiens begin showing up. Just before that, around 10,800 B,C., another disaster devasted the Homo sapiens. The exact cause is unknown, but possibly solar activity, or a sudden bombardment of asteroids, created major impacts that cause ocean levels to rise to 400 ft. and left a black "mat" across North and South America and into Europe. Around 9,600 BC, it happened again, causing a population bottleneck, in terms of their migration. These two events wiped out most of the Mega-Fauna of North and South America and Europe, and all the mammoths, saber-tooth tigers and most of every other type of life over 100 lbs.

Our early ancestors endured a lot of disasters that changed the world, but our species survived. As the population of Homo sapiens developed, groups eventually became towns, which eventually became empires: the Hittite, Babylon, Mycenae Greeks, Assyria and Egypt. Between 1200 and 1100 B.C., a warring group that historians call the "sea people" mostly wiped out these empires, except in Egypt, whose decline was due to the loss of trade. This was the end of the Bronze Age.

In time, empires rose again, Greece, Rome, Celt, Egypt and others. China was isolated, but it had its important Silk Road trade route. Life went on as before, with wars, volcanic eruptions, earthquakes and so on.

Around 1300 A.D., there was a "mini" Ice Age until the middle of 1800 A.D. Once again, ice came out of the North. Life went on as usual, with war, plague, famine, etc. But, in 1453 after an eight-year siege, the Ottoman Empire conquered Constantinople, which cut off trade on the Silk Road with what was left of Europe. Spain's desire to get back to trading with China started the "age of explorers," during which both North and South America were found, beginning in 1492.

Before the Spanish explorers made it to the Americas, there was a large population of Native Americans already living on those continents. Based on the available evidence, scientists believe that 50 to 100 million people lived in the Americas – like the Aztecs, the Mound Builders, and the Incas in South America and many native tribes in North America.
What Spain brought to the Americas was the flu, viruses and Smallpox, which killed close to 85% of the native population, and wiping out whole empires. The depopulation of the land allowed forests to regrow, and huge herds of bison and massive flocks of birds (including passenger pigeons) to thrive, as well.

Once again, European settlers moved in with more of their Smallpox and flu viruses, which killed even more native Americans. This time, though, they brought slaves from Africa with them.

These historic facts are evidence that we are all one big family that started 28 million years ago and is still here today. We are Homo sapiens who have been through a lot of hard times, and almost didn't make it. If it weren't for the Homo sapiens of East Africa who survived the volcanic eruption, we would be an extinct species. In terms of the Homo sapiens species, you may not be who you think you are. Get a DNA test and see your true ancestry for yourself.

Now we get to the time in our history where all of the different groups of Homo sapiens come together: Europeans, Asians, and Africans in one big melting pot: the colonization of America. When Columbus reached the Bahamas is 1492 and landed on San Salvador, he brought African slaves with him. There's not much information about this, but whether or not they helped sail his ships, doesn't matter; they were still slaves. Columbus also enslaved Native Americans, we know that Native Americans' lives didn't matter to him either.

I know I've skipped a lot of history, but as I told you, I'm not writing a book! I am trying to open a conversation about Race issues. Like I said, I'm a 60-year-old white male who works as banquet cook. I've seen a lot of racist stuff in my years. My dad and mom raised me to understand that rich or poor, black, white or brown, we are all equal in deserving fairness and respect.

When the Black Lives Movement started, I thought, 'It's about time!' When I heard the slogan "Black Lives Matter" I asked myself, 'When did black lives ever matter?" I decided to research the history of the human race to find out if their lives ever did matter. Here's what I discovered.

In the 1500's, as America was being colonized, Spain favored areas around Florida. They brought some slaves with them, but most colonists used Native Americans as slaves. However, Native Americans frequently died from the flu and smallpox because they had no immunity to the European diseases which the Spaniards brought with them. By the 1600's, when the Native American population was decimated by death from these diseases, the Spaniards began bringing enslaving Africans to the New World.

Roanoke was the first English settlement in America in 1585. By 1590 everybody had vanished; historians don't know why, but they surmise it was by starvation, disease or Indian attacks. The next colony to start up in Virginia was Jamestown (Fort Monroe) in 1607, where 80 percent of the colonists died of starvation in the winter of 1611. When the colony was back on its feet, the first African slaves arrived in Jamestown (Fort Monroe), in August of 1619 on the pirate ship, "The White Lion." 20 slaves that had been taken as bounty from an English ship were bought by the settlers. None of their names were recorded, so their identities are lost to history. Most of the slaves brought to Jonestown at that time were treated as indentured servants.

There was another land grab in the Americas, before the Homestead Act. In the 1500's most of the slavers were Native Americans, but they kept dying of disease, etc., and had to be continually replaced. In the early 1600's, the British began the *Head Right System,* which was, if you didn't have the money to America, you could sign up as an indentured servant for a plantation owner or farmer for 5 to 7 years; at the end of that period, you'd get 50 acres of land – mostly Native American land. By 1619, former African indentured servants started arriving in the West to claim their property.

Another provision of the Head Right System was that for each slave an American owner bought he got 50 free acres; so the more slaves he bought, the more land he got. After 5-7 years, as many of the indentured servants got their 50 acres, they left the plantations. By then, there was a large indentured servant population. They became increasingly resentful of their treatment by owners, and that some were not given the land they were promised at the end of their indentured time period. The result was the Bacon's Rebellion of 1676.

After Jamestown was burned to the ground, the colonists enacted new laws that declared their slaves as their property, including their child and took the 50 acres promised the slaves for themselves. The total acreage given to, or taken by, white Europeans in America between the Homestead Act and the Head Right System, is anyone's guess.

Between 1619 and 1639, African slaves were treated like indentured servants. they could buy their freedom and buy property and had a few "freedoms." Then, after the laws of 1639 and all the ones after that, it went from kind of bad to very bad and kept getting worse. The long, cruel history of American slavery was well on its way.

The cultivation of tobacco started around 1612 and around the same time, in the Caribbean, sugar cane farms got bigger. When 1620 rolled around, many of these farms had turned into Plantations, and the need for more African slaves increased. And on it goes.

At this time, African slaves could buy their freedom, own property or slaves, themselves. But 50 years later, in 1672, by law slaves were no longer people. They were property, and if you had a problem with them, you could kill them.

Cotton soon kicked in as a big crop and more slaves were needed in the cotton fields. The more slaves a plantation owner had, the more he felt the need to keep control of them.
As African slaves became a large population in America, and only way to control them, owners believed, was through fear, maintained by physical and psychological brutality.

In late 1630, the colonies passed "black laws" in order to distinguish indentured servants from African slaves. In 1639 a law was passed saying that even if a slave is baptized, he is still a slave; inter-racial sex and marriage were banned; Africans were deprived of property and could not bear arms, and slaves could not travel without the permission of their owners. In 1669, a law was passed making it legal to kill an unruly slave. In 1672 another law made it legal to wound or kill slaves that resisted arrest. In 1692 they were denied a jury trial and could not own horses, hogs or cattle. Most of these "black laws" also applied to Native Americans. These law were an attempt to reinforce the social values of the time – a set of rules that regulated human conduct, according to the "will of the people."

So killing, whipping and maiming them was the way to terrorize the slaves, intended to discourage their rebelliousness. It seems that Black Lives Didn't matter, and the same goes for Native Americans. So ends the 1600's.

Thus, Africans, the only full-blooded Homo sapiens on earth, with no Neanderthal DNA, became regarded as a "sub-human" species in America, and other places, where slavery was part of "doing business."

In the early 1700's conditions for slaves remained poor and they still lived in fear. Then revolts started happening. Over the next 150 years, there were something like 250 slave revolts. There is some debate about the number, but the end result is the same. The plantation owners got scared and paranoid, which meant even more brutality, more torture and more killing. Families were split up. Slaves were lynched, set on fire and their hands and limbs were cut off. This was usually done in front of plantation slaves because their aim was to control the slaves, both physically and mentally. Fear is a powerful weapon and the slave owners used it to the max. Most of these atrocities happened on the plantations and super plantations.

There were also small family farms at the time who used slaves. The smaller farmers probably treated their slaves a little better. I can't find much information about how small farm owners treated their slaves, but I'm thinking that this might be how the legend of the "happy slave" got started. Many small farm owners had only two or three slaves who helped them operate their farms. They probably had better living conditions than the slaves on plantations; we do know that some small-farm slaves had their own houses, food, and clothing, for instance.

As time went by, the slave revolts continued happening. In 1775, when the Revolutionary War began, more than 5,000 African men, some "free" and some slaves, fought bravely and with honor alongside the colonists against the British. After the War, some Northern states made slavery against the law, but slave ownership still existed in some Northern states up to the time of the Civil War, though conditions did get a little better for Africans in the Northern states.

In the South, things got worse. Laws were passed to stop slaves from running away to flee to the north. Slaves that fought for the British in the war were sent back or sold to sugar cane plantations in the Caribbean for $1,000 each. Around this same time, Native Americans were dying of the flu and smallpox. Whole Indian tribes were wiped out, along with their cultures.

When the French Revolution began in 1789, the slaves on a little French-occupied island in the Caribbean, Hispaniola/Saint Domingo (now called Haiti), revolted and began kicking the French off the island. This made American plantation owners nervous. In an effort to stop plantation slaves from escaping, their travel was restricted and brutality against them increased.

When Eli Whitney invented the Cotton Gin to remove cotton seeds in 1793, it was very important for the cotton industry. Cotton could not be processed with its seeds, and removing the seeds was a very time-consuming task, so more slaves were needed in the fields. Cotton plantation owners brought more slaves from Africa, and also shipped them down the river from Northern states to their cotton plantations. By the end of the 1700's Black Lives still didn't matter. They were valued only for their work, but not as human beings. Native Americans were also demeaned, not seen as people, but as 'animals" and "savages." Their Lives didn't matter either.

By the start of the 1800's the slave revolt in Haiti was over. After they beat the French army, the Spanish army and the British army, when Napoleon sent another army to recapture Haiti, they were beaten, too. You can guess what happened next. American plantation owners started a new campaign of relentless terror and abuse, in an attempt to control their own slaves.

Few people in America in the 1700's and 1800's could read, so newspapers at that time often used "cartoons" depicting news events. Many of the drawings depicted African slaves as "sub-human," being degraded and abused by their owners. Over the decades, they probably contributed to the "dehumanizing" of slaves in the minds of the white population. That image gained a lot of traction when, in 1836, a white performer, Jim Crow, hit the stage as a minstrel caricature of an African man.

The number of enslaved Africans increased every year in the U.S. In 1763, the slave population was around 230,000. By 1860, a hundred years later, there were around 4 million slaves in America.

Jim Crow was a white actor named, Thomas Dartmouth Rice who dressed up as an African slave who acted dumb and clumsy and spoke in a way that mocked the African race. The show became a huge hit across the U.S. and Britain. At the same time, the Ku Klux Klan started terrorizing African communities. That was bad, but then came an even crueler blow, that still affects attitudes toward African-Americans today – Charles Darwin's biggest mistake: his *scientific racism* theory described in his 1859 book, *The Descent of Man.* It purported to show that through natural selection, this "scientific" theory had been taking place over hundreds or thousands of years.

Darwin's book brought this theory to mainstream science, and many scientists jumped on the band wagon. The theory was that different races were different species that races developed independently of each other; and that the African race was naturally closer to apes. It even claimed that Irish people were a non-white race, and that civilized societies were harming humanity by helping the poor, sick and disabled, who nature would have killed off, to survive. The physically weaker, the less intelligent and the morally lower." Helping these people goes against the Laws of Natural Selection, and this was the main problem with Darwin's theory in *The Descent of Man.* The theory was supported by the newspapers, scientists and universities and it took off. It was taught in schools up to World War II. Some people put Africans in zoos and sideshows as main attractions, "Come See the Ape Man." The USA and Germany ran with this theory until a British scholar developed another theory, call *eugenics* (meaning "well-born,") in the early 1900's (more on this theory later).

So, back to the timeline –

On April 4, 1861, Abraham Lincoln was inaugurated as the 16th president of the United States. In this span of history, the Republican Party kind of "morphed" into what we think of today as the Democratic Party and helped African Americans as best they could up to the Great Depression. The Democrats of 1860, on the other hand, were more or less White Supremacists until the end of the 19th century, when the Party's conservative and progressive factions clashed over expanding the role of government in enforcing social justice, which gradually became its new identity several decades later. I know it's more complicated than that, but in a nutshell, that's what happened. Again, I invite you to fact-check anything I say.

After Lincoln's election in 1860, The Democrats, now the "Jeffersonians" who believed that commerce, rather than agriculture, was the best way forward, and believed in a weak federal government, controlled both the House and The Senate; the Republicans, mostly Federalists who wanted "big government" and leadership by the wealthy, had the President. White supremacists were strong politically in both the North and the South, and there were a few Abolitionists, who wanted to end slavery outright in America.

By February 1861, the Confederated States of American was born. Confederates attacked five Federal arsenals and five Forts, and the newspapers in the South fanned the flames for war. By March 4, the South was in flames and on April 12, 1861, Fort Sumter was attacked. The war was on. African slaves continued to be terrorized and treated inhumanly. Even in the North, Africans were often treated badly, attacked and terrorized.

After 200 years of slavery, there was now some hope. The southern states that seceded, had no vote in Congress. Lincoln easily passed the Homestead Act of 1862; for a $10 filing fee, if you were an American, or in the process of becoming an American, you would get 160 acres of free land. Over 270 million acres of land was given away through the Homestead Act. African Americans got about eight percent of the land grants, and West they went. Of course,

White Supremacists were migrating West, too. After a few years of organized raids that killed many African-American homesteaders, probably far fewer of the eight percent survived on their land.

In 1862, with the Southern states gone, Lincoln's executive order created The Emancipation Proclamation, and on December 6, 1865 the 13th Amendment was ratified, freeing the slaves. Lincoln was assassinated on April 14, 1865, a few days after the Civil War had ended on April 9.

Lincoln's successor, Andrew Johnson, pretty much a White Supremacist, got the like-minded governors and legislators together and started getting the country "back to order." The South had a big problem: plantation owners had no slaves, and that meant there was no one to work the crops.

Let's talk *share-cropping* – a way devised by plantation owners to make up for the loss of their slave labor. Share-cropping meant that a person "leased" a plot of land from the owner, and then after growing and harvesting the crop, shared it with the landowner. In the South, black people did not have tools or seeds (or a home, for that matter), so landowners supplied them for a "cost." After the harvest, the landowner would take those "cost" out of the sharecroppers' portion of the harvest, leaving the sharecropper with very little. The plantation owner was able to do this because between 1500 up to the late 1700's all slaves bought off the slave ships via the Head Right System was worth 50 acres. The white Europeans acquired a lot of land from that system. The sharecroppers were legally "freed" but they were still slaves.

Cotton was the number one crop of the economy, the plantations still needed workers. So, the southern states looked for a loophole in the law, and the found it in the 13th Amendment. Yes, it freed all men and women and ended slavery in America, but there was one clause they could use in their favor – that a convicted person can still be subjected to involuntary servitude. In other words, if you get sent to jail, you could be considered a slave. In 1865 and 1866, southern governors started making Laws known as the Black Code, which were intended to help plantation owners.

Black Code laws legalized black marriages. Black people could own land with restrictions. They could go to court and testify, but only against other blacks. They could not vote, they could not own firearms, and there were many other laws that restricted the freedom of ex-slaves. Most significant, though, were the vagrancy laws, which said that all black adults must sign a labor contract with a white employer for one year. Without a contract, you were a vagrant; even if you had your own farm and no contract you were a vagrant and sent to jail. According to the 13th Amendment you were then considered a slave. You would be fined and if you couldn't pay it, the courts would auction off the prisoner to pay the fine; it usually took a year or more to pay back the fine to the plantation owner. In this way, plantation owners got much of their work force back.

The Black Codes in the south did not go over well with the northern states. They had just fought a four-year war to end slavery, and they were not going to let this Black Code reinstate slavery. So, they passed the 14th Amendment, which gave citizenship and equal protection under the law to ex-slaves. That meant no more auctioning off of inmates to pay their fines. But, the plantation owners still needed workers, so the southern state courts and police came up with the idea of *work gangs* for the plantations. With the clause in the 13th amendment still in force, the police could still pick up a black person on any charge and when the courts convicted them, off to work on the plantation they'd go. This practice is still going on! How? What is the difference, you might ask, between the *work gangs* of the past and today's jail and prison *work crews* doing all the cooking and cleaning in most of our jails and prisons? Check out the facts for yourself, folks.

You might also ask: Why does the U.S. have the largest prison population in the world?

After the slaves were freed in 1865, a lot of them went looking for family members or other relatives who were taken away while they were slaves. So, there are all these ex-slaves wandering around the country looking for their brothers and sisters, etc., and you have the southern police and courts looking for laborers for the plantations. It did not work out well for the ex-slaves.

Before the war ended, Lincoln asked what the slaves want, they replied: land and tools. So after the war, Lincoln was going to give the slaves 40 acres and a mule right after the war. When Lincoln was killed, and Johnson became president, that deal never happened. Ex-slaves never got any land or a mule.

due to the combination of sharecropping and the numbers of "vagrants" rounded up by the Southern police and courts that ended up back on the plantations, the economy of the south was starting to come back. Even with the Northern Union Army enforcing the 13 and 14th Amendments across the south. Black people were still having a hard time voting, and so on.

On February 3, 1870, the 15th Amendment was ratified – that gave all men (but not women) in the U S the right to Vote. The 14th Amendment only protected citizens' civil rights, not their political rights. The 15th Amendment protected political rights. This did not go over well with the white supremacists and they had a plan.

In December of 1865, six Confederate veterans who had been members of the Knights of the Golder Circle (KGC) got together in Pulaski, Tennessee and formed a new secret society. The KGC had been outlawed after the Civil War, so they renamed it, using the words *Ku Klux* supposedly derived from the Greek word *kyklos,* meaning circle, and Klan by changing the letter "c" in the Scottish word, *clan,* to a K. One of their "rules" was that you had to wear a costume – a robe, mask and hood (presumably to heighten their fear factor). Their purpose was to intimidate "Carpetbaggers" (a derogatory term Confederates called Northerners who came to the South) and to terrorize newly freed slaves.

There were other violent groups made up of former Confederate soldiers at that time, seeking to push back against reconstruction policies. In 1867 a former Confederate general and slave trader, Nathan Bedford Forrest, brought all the groups together into a national organization, with a new goal of fighting against the civil rights granted by the 13th 14th and 15th amendments. So, if you were black and not working on a plantation or a farm with a white owner (who could protect you), you had a target on your back.

These groups went around the countryside in their costumes and hoods, terrorizing black people at night. They shot into houses and burned them down, sometimes with the occupants still inside. They targeted black farmers and black businesses and any black man who tried to vote. They organized political rallies that turned into riots, the causes of which were always obscured.

The Freedmen's Bureau, created to help former slaves transition from being a slave to being emancipated, building hospitals, banks, and over 1,000 schools for African-American children, reported that thousands of black people were murdered. Even with the Northern army in the South, the brutality continued. These terror groups believed they had to beat down African-Americans, both physically and psychologically, in order to control them. They aimed to degrade, demoralize and terrorize them in order to demonstrate their dominance and authority.

Around this time, Darwin's Theory of "scientific racism," proposing that different races were actually different subspecies of Homo sapiens, is beginning to show up in schoolbooks and in major universities in the U.S. and Europe.

In the late 1870's Wilmington, the largest city in North Carolina, had a majority black population – about 55% of a population of 25,000. There were many black businessmen and a rising middle class. Many had skills that they could use in the marketplace, making up to 35% of the city's service positions, and 30% of the city's craftsmen, and over 2,000 professionals, like lawyers, doctors and clergymen. Blacks were elected to local office and gained prominent positions in the community, like Justice of the Peace, police and many others. There were black-owned restaurants and most of the barbers. Generally, whites and blacks in the city got along pretty well, but there were some problems, such as bank loans, property issues and taxes. The KKK sometimes put on their costumes and terrorized the countryside, burning down churches and houses, lynching and torturing black citizens. But, in this city, it was better than it had been for 260 years, excluding the Southern states during reconstruction that lasted about 12 years, to 1877. Then Jim Crow laws took over.

After winning the 1894 state election, the republicans started dismantling the racist laws and rules of the Democratic Party. That upset the white supremacists. After that, a "white supremacy campaign" – really a political campaign, got started. In the 1896 election, however, the Democrats lost all of their statewide power. Black candidates were winners throughout North Carolina. This was bad for the Democrats, but the white supremacists were "freaking out" too. They got together and made a plan for the 1898 election. They believed the only way to win was to find ways to stop black people from voting. So, they started up again with their lynching and terrorizing tactics.

They asked the KKK for their help, but the KKK had been outlawed with the Act of 1870, and backed it up with the KKK Act 4/20/1871 and 1870. Because of that law, they put their costumes in the closet and put on red shirts and became a paramilitary pat of the Democratic Party. They got in the newspapers and the political cartoonists helped out and that brought in the national media fanning the flames of hate; and let's not forget the noise in the background – Darwin's Theory of Scientific Racism.

All these forces were working against the black population of North Carolina, and by this point in time, The Republicans had sent four black representatives to Congress, so the state has a total of 11 black representatives in the House. Black people were beginning to become a part of the government, so everything was getting ready for the November 8 state election.

The Red Shirts (a white supremacist paramilitary group) terrorized the black community not to vote, and the political cartoonists aided and abetted their cause. When it came time to vote, however, black men did show up to vote and the white supremacist did not gain control of the city or the state. The next day the Democrats gave the leaders of the city a document called, "The White Declaration of Independence." The day after that, the white supremacists, the

Democrats and the Red Shirts marched on The Daily Record, the only black newspaper in North Carolina. The newspaper owner, Alex Manly, had responded to a column about lynching by saying that, 'Although every negro lynched is called a "big burly black brute," in fact, many were sufficiently attractive for white girls of culture and refinement to fall in love with them,' which pissed off the white supremacists.

The next thing this crowd of over 2,000 white supremacists did was shoot every black person they could find. They even brought a Gatling gun. While the killing on the streets is going on, about 200 armed men showed up at the Courthouse and forced the Mayor and his Aldermen to resign; they were kicked out of the city and told that if they returned, they would be killed. The Democrats took over Wilmington. A Raleigh newspaper reporting on the killings said the forest was "black with the hanging black bodies." The bodies were never counted, and no one was charged in the massacre.

The federal government did nothing; and to understand why, we need to know about the Colfax Riot of 1873. During Reconstruction in the south black people were able to run for office and vote, so they started running for office again and registering to vote.

In Colfax, Louisiana, in 1873, the Republican party won the election, but the Democratic party wanted to steal the election for themselves. The Republicans went to the Courthouse to take over their election positions. The first attack on the courthouse was on April 3, 1873 and the second attack was on April 5, 1873. The black community helped defend the courthouse on Easter Sunday, April 13, 1873 during a major attack by the crowd, but the Republicans surrendered and were then murdered – over 150 black people. The aftermath of that was that three white supremacists were convicted of the crimes. But their convictions were appealed to the Supreme Court, which said in United States vs. Cruikshank (1876) that the protection of the 14th Amendment did not apply to the actions of individuals, but only to the actions of the state governments. This ruling by the Supreme Court nullified the Enforcement Act of 1870 and the KKK laws of 1871, which made it possible for groups like the white supremacists, KKK, the Knights of the White Camelia, red shirts and so on, to form and become the paramilitary groups they are today throughout the U.S.A.

So, back to Wilmington – that is why no one was convicted of the courthouse massacre. For that to happen, the state would have had to file charges, which means that the Republicans would have had to take over the state government. Instead, survivors of the Wilmington massacre came out of the forest and graveyards, and along with thousands of other members of the black community, left their homes, property, farms and businesses behind, grabbed what they could, and fled, like a flock of geese, across the U.S. to join African-American communities in other states. Their tales were told around campfires, added to all the other tales told about the inhumane way whites had treated them. The tales went from generation to generation. Young children were told never look the White Man in the eye, hold your head down and do not defy him, because he will hunt you and kill you – just as the parents were told by their parents.

So we come to the end of the 1800's. The situation at this time was that after slavery was abolished, a lot of southern states had larger numbers of free African-Americans than white people. So, the whites got out and voted in every election. Since the white supremacists knew how to keep African-Americans from voting, they used their fear and terror techniques to show their white dominance and authority, once again. They invaded black communities and massacred many black citizens. These killings were not only motivated by keeping them from voting, but also by the hatred and other grievances whites had again blacks. Between 1865 and 1900, thousands of black people were lynched or otherwise murdered in the south and in other parts of the U.S., too.

By the 1900's in America, African-Americans are still living in fear of "the white man." Since I'm not writing a book, I've had to skip over a lot of things, like many more lynchings and massacres of black citizens, and a couple of wars on U.S. soil. You can find a list of the many race-related riots and massacres that took place between the 19th and 2lst centuries, in the Appendix, at the end of this piece.

In the 20th century quite a bit of progress was made in terms of African-American self-sufficiency, including a growing number of skilled and better-educated communities and the establishment of many African-American enterprises.

I hope you will be motivated to do your own research on this and every other time period discussed in these pages. As I said previously, please fact-check yourself anything you read here. Much of the history of Africans in America was unknown to me until I started researching it.

Regarding the wars on U.S. soil, many black citizens stood up, ready and willing to fight for their country, and they fought with bravery and honor, even though often being segregated and treated badly.

In the presidential election of 1876, you had Rutherford B. Hayes and Samuel Tilden. Tilden was a Democrat who disputed the theory of Evolution, along with white supremacists in Louisiana, Florida and. South Carolina. The Republicans were trying to help black people. Tilden won the popular vote, but Hayes won the electoral vote, so they came up with a compromise: Tilden would give the presidency to Hayes if he would pull all the Union troops out of the South and stay out of southern politics – it was called The Compromise of 1877. So, Hayes became president and the troops pulled out, ending Reconstruction in the South. At this point, the U.S. government gave up on racial equality for African-Americans. Southern Democrats took political control of the South and right away "Jim Crow laws" went into effect throughout the South. As mentioned previously, Jim Crow was a fictitious African slave character portrayed by Thomas Rice, a white actor, as dumb and clumsy. This mockery of the African-American race was a huge hit across the U.S. and Britain. "Jim Crow" as a derogatory term for African-Americans, was attached to racial segregation laws and practices in the U.S.

Since each state made their own laws, "Jim Crow states" were easy to spot, and segregation was their number one priority. They legalized the separate use of public facilities and accommodations like schools, transportations, bathrooms and shop, and created other restrictions that made it harder for African-Americans to vote, own land, access education, firearms, and so on. In response, black communities established their own schools, stores, hotels, churches, water fountains, etc. When it came to voting, though, a black man had to pay a vote tax and pass an intelligence test first. If he actually did get to vote, the KKK would come looking for him. The black community put up with this for a while, but as time went by, things began to change.

A man named Ernst Haeckel, a zoologist from Germany, considered one of their top scientists, was a big supporter of Darwin. He studied medicine and spent part of 1866-67 with Darwin in the Canary Island while Darwin was writing *The Descent of Man*, which came out in 1871. He returned to German and began writing "Theory of Scientific Reason" and came up with 12 Homo sapiens "sub-species" and each one of them had 4 genus and that meant that Homo sapiens had 48 sub-species, which meant that the Anglo Saxon who are on top of the evolution Chart, had to worry about who they mated with, because their offspring cold become an evolutionary throwback. The intellectual and elites wanted something done, so enter Eugenics. By 1916, Germany with the help of Ernst Heckel, started the political ideology that would last until after WWII. The newspapers and the political cartoonists started to pick this up and the "threat of the subhuman" was news. All around the world people wanted something done because more criminal and degenerates and sub-humans are out breeding the elite in this struggle for existence. The wrong people are winning out, so they need to rectify this situation. Eugenics was the answer. This was going on in the US and around the world. So in July of 1933, when the Nazis came into power within six months, they passed a law of compulsory sterilization for those who were considered physically or mentally handicapped – especially those who were "a burden to society." They sterilized several hundred thousand people in a short amount of time. Then starting on October 1939, after WWII, they started a *euthanasia* program that killed more than 70,000 mentally and physically handicapped people. While Germany took the path of extermination, the US took the path of sterilization.

Sterilization advocates were influenced by the popular "science" of the time, which was actually a collection of unproved theories, including Darwinism, that seemed say it would be a good idea to eliminate the "undesirable elements" from the human race. However, scientific knowledge at that time, did not include an understanding of how the "mechanics" of heredity actually works.

In 1907, Indiana became the first state to enact a compulsory sterilization laws. Most criminals and by 1935, 41 states did too. And it was not just criminals. Now it was also mentally ill and disabled people. Believe it or not, legal sterilizations, disproportionately including black men and women, continued after WW II in the USA. The program slowed down a little when President Nixon started a program that involved women on Welfare. If you wanted to be on Welfare, you had to get sterilized and by the time that program ended, 400,000 people were sterilized, mostly women of color. Legal Eugenics stayed around until 1984, but the theory of Eugenics is still around today. Between 1907 and 1984, 470,000 to 480,000 people were sterilized in the US.

Now that we're in the 1900's, we need to talk about the political shifts of the Republican Party and the Democratic Party in America. This is a bit complicated, so I will simplify it by omitting some of the nuances of the ideologies. For the sake of this discussion, I will call them "Might Makes Right" and "The Meek Shall Inherit the Earth." "Might Makes Right" is like war, chaos and innovation; while "The Meek Shall Inherit the Earth" is like peace, helping each other and stagnation. If you look back through history, both systems fail. But two ideologies with their different interests forced to work together and meet in the middle, seems to work.

Historically, the pendulum of power swings back and forth between "Might Makes Right" to "The Meek Shall Inherit the Earth." When it comes to African-Americans and Native Americans, you could say the pendulum has gotten stuck on the "Might Makes Right" side.

At the end of the 1900's you have the Civil War over for 35 years. The Republican Party is working with African-Americans and the Democrats are supporting the white supremacists. After the Wilmington massacre, you don't hear much about white supremacists as a political group, but more about individuals or small groups claiming to be the "White Supremacist Party." However, the white supremacy movement continued to be supported by groups like the KKK and Red Shirts.

Around this time, the U.S. government has taken all of the Native Americans' land, which they were giving away to settlers, and you also had boats full of immigrants coming to the U.S. from all over Europe. At this time, the Republican Party was becoming pro-business. In 1912, for the first time since the Civil War, a Democrat was elected president; the 28th president of the U.S., Woodrow Wilson. During his eight years in office, he replaced the Central Bank with the 1914 Federal Trade Commission. The Federal Reserve system started to segregate the Federal workforce, sending African Americans to letter-job positions.

The screening of "Birth of a Nation" in 1915, thus legitimized the movie and that rebooted the KKK. By 1925, 4 million Americans had become members of the KKK.

During Wilson's last term, the U.S got into WW I on April 6, 1917, until November 11, 1918. In 1919 he passed the 18th and 19th amendments. The 18th Amendment was Prohibition and lasted until 1933; the 19th amendment was the vote for women. In the last three years of his term, lynching of African-Americans was a big problem, but he did nothing.

In 1919 the Red Summer Riots were going on and hundreds of African-Americans were being killed and their communities destroyed. Wilson did nothing, so in the 1920 election, the Republican Party took back the presidency and continued to be pro-business, and less labor-friendly. In the meantime, the Democrats are starting to make social reforms and being Labor-friendly.

By 1929 the Great Depression hit and President Herbert Hoover, a Republican believer in minimal government intervention, did little to help the American people.

By 1932, 11 million people were out of work, and half of U.S. banks failed. In 1932, Franklin Delano Roosevelt, a Democrat, became president. In his first 100 days in office, he passed a lot of legislation, which he called The New Deal. It created agencies like the WPA (Works Progress Administration) and National Recovery Administration that focused on creating jobs that put money into the hands of working people. In 1936, he created the Social Security Administration and pensions for elderly Americans. These economic reforms caused African-Americans to start voting Democratic ticket in U.S. elections.

The Depression ended when we entered WW II. When the war was over in 1945, the G.I. bill was passed giving a benefits packs for all returning servicemen. The package included cash, help with college tuition for vocational education and trade schools + very low interest mortgages, which helped 1.2 million veterans. However, in states where there were Jim Crow laws, African-Americans got a lot less help than white veterans. Banks wouldn't loan them money and they were not allowed to attend segregated white schools. So, just as with the Homestead Act and the Head Right System, African-Americans were at the bottom on the list for receiving help from the GI Bill in the South. Take a look at List of Riots for these years, at the end of this writing.

In 1954, Brown v. Board of Education overruled the 1896 Supreme Court Decision of Plessy v. Ferguson, that legalized segregation under the "separate but equal" rule. Segregation was now illegal in the United States of America. This opened the door for the Civil Rights Act of 1964.

The Republican Party in the 1960's remained pro-business and against social reform, and the Democrats were pro-labor and pro-social reform. In 1964, the Democrats passed the Civil Rights Act. The KKK went over to the Republican Party, and more riots ensued in the 1960's – look them up on the List of Riots at the end of this writing.

The depression ended between 1930 and 1960. I think of it as a "musical chairs" era, when the lines of liberal and conservative ideologies got blurred. Towards the end of the Depression, the priorities of the political parties began to changes. This started the music playing. It got people moving from party to party; African-Americans began leaving the Republican Party, and the racists within the Democratic party weren't happy with African-Americans coming into their party so they switched over to the Republican Party. This game of musical chairs lasted for 30 to 50 years. Since that time, both parties are equally mixed with a spectrum of political views, which has helped pass some great bills through the legislature.

In the 70's, the police departments became unionized. This was good and bad, in that although police are heroes every day across this country, and risk their lives, the integrity of police departments is tainted by individual officers who are violent, racist, or abuse their powers. Police departments say wants them gone, but the Police Union fights and lies to keep them on the police force – no matter how bad one is or how many times he shoots innocent suspects. The Police Union formed in the 1970's, over 40 years. How many "rotten apples" are still spoiling the bushel of apples? It is the police unions that have compromised the integrity of the both the departments and the individual members of the unions around the country. It is the Union that has caused the public to lose trust in the police. Trust is an easy thing to lose – it doesn't take much, but it is a hard thing to re-establish. Trust has to be earned.

Check out the riots of the 1960's in the attached list of riots. How many of those protests were because a member of the black community was killed by a police officer, who eventually went unpunished for killing or seriously injuring members of the black community. How many of those protests turned into riots because the police attacked the protesters and set off a riot. This is the same playbook they used in the 1800's. So, we hear what they say, but more importantly we see what they do.

In the 1980's we still had police killing African-Americans without any real consequences or punishment because the Unions protected them with what they call "qualified immunity," even though many people protested the lack of punishment. Then, when the Police started attacking protesters, the news reporters called it a riot. This is a pattern that worked in the 1960's and 70's and it is still at play today.

In 1953, a scientist named Rosalind Franklin took the first photograph of a DNA double helix strand, which started intense DNA research over the next four decades. In 1989, scientists started the Human Genome Project, which was a map of our DNA (Deoxyribose-nucleic Acid) in human cells. There are about 3 billion base pairs. The mapping took 13 years to finish, and fundamentally changed the way science thinks about genetics and heredity.

We now know that 99.96% of all genetic material is the same in all Homo sapiens. This means that Homo sapiens did not develop independently of each other, and that different races are not different species. It means that Darwin's theory of "scientific racism" was flat-out wrong. How many people were killed because of belief of this baseless theory of white (Caucasian) superiority over Africans, and how many Jews did the Germans kill because of their political ideology that was based on the erroneous belief that there was such a thing as a "pure race." This has been going on for hundreds of years, families teaching their children generation after generation (and some still do), virtually brainwashing their children that white supremacy is a fact, rather than fiction. How do we stop this?

They found something else during the Genome Project. They traced human ancestry back 150,000 years and discovered something astounding: 150,000 years ago there was just one original group of Homo sapiens on earth, and they lived in Eastern Africa. Then, about 60,000 years ago, when some Homo sapiens began migrating out of African, they interbred with Neanderthals, a humanoid species that pre-dates Homo sapiens by a 200,000 years. Since most of the world's human population (past and present) have Neanderthal DNA, *except* for Native Africans in both East and West Africa, who have *no* Neanderthal DNA, Native Africans are the only human beings on earth with a pure-blood lineage as Homo sapiens!

This scientific discovery is not good news for white supremacists, since it means that they, too, along with their ancestors, came out of Africa like everyone else.

False information has misled many people for the last 400 years. There is no sub-human race. There is no such thing as racial "devolving" and the "scientific racism theory" is false. We are all part of the same species – Homo sapiens.

I know what racism is, I just don't understand *why* it is so pervasive in American society. Why have white people had so much hatred toward black people that it compelled them to terrorize, brutalize and murder African-Americans over the centuries from the country's very beginning with no remorse? I can understand, though, why African-American citizens, and others, have continually railed against systemic racism in American society.

What have African-Americans done to merit the wrath of so many white Americans who has mistreated, demeaned, ostracized and relegated to second-class status behind them, or worse. Hmmm…let's See – what have Africans and African-American citizens done to America, anyway:

- They helped build this country from its earliest years.
- Their labor on plantations helped start America's great economy.
- They helped build America's roads, towns, cities and national parks.
- They fought courageously in every U.S. war.
- African-American athletes have taken our sports teams to the heights of success.
- The collective creative talent of African-Americans musicians, artists and writers have enlightened and enriched American culture.

Why are Americans so less tolerant and accepting of other cultures and traditions. Why do so many of us think that we are "superior" because our skin color is lighter, or because we have better jobs or education or more money than other races.

Racism is not something we are born with – it is learned, taught by our parents, and white-bias is taught in our schools through biased history books, incomplete histories that are taught to kids.

Even with "racism" entrenched in American society, we have a responsibility, as citizens to lessen its impact and the toll it takes on the lives of African-Americans and other races who live and work in the U.S. and contribute their best efforts, give of them for their betterment of our society and the individual people in it.

Even given the reality that people aren't going to stop being prejudice or feeling superior to others or hating certain groups of people, they still do not have the right to "act out" on these feelings by harming, banning or passing laws against people they don't like.

Even the slaves of ancient Rome, had more rights and freedoms than American slaves – for example, there were laws against killing slaves.

In the 1500's Slavery because a big business. Called the Atlantic Slave trade. It started between the Portuguese Colonies of West Africa and the Spanish Settlement of the Caribbean's and Americas. The Spanish sugar cane plantations in the Caribbean needed laborers, and Native Americas were dying off from diseases, and indentured servants were dying off from Yellow Fever and tropical diseases. Africans had immunity to European diseases and little problem with tropical diseases, so the Portuguese met with the African tribal Chiefs and traded guns and alcohol with them for the tribes' slaves. This is how the Atlantic Slave trade got started.

Slavery has been around for thousands of years. In the beginning it was the product of war, when prisoners of war were put into slavery. There are different kinds of slavery, so let's break it down into categories of Domestic and Industrial. Domestic slaves would include farmhands, housemaids, etc., and Industrial slaves would be mining, road building, etc., which was more of a punishment for not being cooperative. Ancient empires had rules for slave-owners, and laws that protected slaves; and slaves could buy their freedom. By 1450 A.D., slavery was dying out, leaving mostly domestic servants. During the time of the Portuguese colonies in West Africa, the gold mines started to dry up, and in the Caribbean, the Spanish settlements were having a labor shortage problem due to the fact that their native workers were dying off from diseases like yellow fever and malaria. They had a new crop of sugar cane to harvest and high demand for it.

When the Portuguese discovered that African slaves had better immunity to diseases, they began making deals with African tribes to trade guns, ammunition, alcohol and other goods in exchange for some of their slaves. By 1480, slave ships were going to Cape Verde and the Madeira Islands, and before long, sugar cane plantations were thriving all over the Caribbean. As the Atlantic Slave Trade was taking off, the Dutch, English and French, etc., starting setting up their own slave gathering settlements in Africa. When they de-populated an area in Africa, they moved to another area and started up again.

Soon, tribes were fighting tribes and Africa had its own arms race. This went on between 1480 and 1880. The last slave ship, called the Clotilda, left for America in 1880, and over 20 million Africans were kidnapped from their homes to become slaves around the world. You might wonder what the churches and religious institutions were doing about this. Well, they used Bible scriptures to propagate slavery, such as Genesis 9:24:23 – Ham, the son of Noah, was cursed by Noah and then in Genesis 10 the "Table of Nations" describes the origins of the different races and reveals that one of descendants of Ham is Cush, and the Cushites were people from North Africa in the Nile region. So they say that all Africans were descendants of Ham and their skin was dark because Noah cursed Ham and all of his descendants. Using other Bible scripture and preaching good behavior like, "Obey your master" and "Be a good slave," all around the world as a justification for slavery and sowed the seeds of racism. We now know that these stories are wrong because of the Genome Project. For 500 years these false religious ideas, backed up by Darwin's *Theory of the Descent of Man*, was the perfect storm for dehumanizing an entire race, triggered, for the most part, by the need for laborers for sugar harvesting.

African tribes had slaves, themselves, which they acquired from winning wars, and they were treated relatively well – such as domestic slaves who were part of the tribal societies.

So slavery is not something that was devised or invented in America. However, the brutality and terror and killings in America was unlike their homeland. So this new kind of slavery was something the world hadn't experiences previously.

As the Spanish plantations got the slaves they needed, the slavers looked for new markets for their slaves.

In August 1619, four days after the White Lion sold 10 slave in Jamestown, the ship, Treasurer, landed with 32 slaves. For every slave bought, the British government gave that new slave-owner 50 or more acres of land. This was the start of American slavery and American racism. There were slave revolts between 1619 and 1863. The riots between 1865 -1946 were about mobs of whites attacking African communities. A list of those riots and the deaths and injuries they caused at the end of this writing.

We have only learned the Genome Project information in the last half a century. Now we know for sure that we are all Homo sapiens – one species. We now know that for the last 450 years, we have been misled by both church doctrine and inaccurate science.

European churches justified the Atlantic slave trade by saying Africans were less human than us, and that we must help them find God and become more "civilized" like us. Then, you had a lot of people believing Darwin's *Theory of the Descent of Man* in the 19th century, which lead to the false notion of "scientific racism," which led to Eugenics, which led to the policy of sterilizing U.S. citizens they deemed "defective" and to Germany turning that falsehood into a political ideology and using it to justify their murdering of millions of people. Even after WWII sterilization in the U.S. continued in the Southern states and prisons.

Now, in 2020, protesters across the country, supported by the Black Lives Matter organization, are fighting for the same thing African-Americans have been fighting for over the last 450 years – to stop the violence and killing of innocent African Americans citizens.

We are likely to start colonizing Mars in the next 20 to 30 years, yet we are still dealing with the cruelty and inhumanity of racial prejudice. Let's grow up, acknowledge our errors as a society, and leave this ugly chapter of America's behavior to the records of history.

Regarding reforms of our police departments – it is going to take a lot of deep changes to move forward in a positive direction. First, many of our police officers are the country's heroes. They risk their lives every day trying to keep us safe, and for the most part, they do – and I am thankful for that.

Police departments are like a big family in some ways , and as in every family, you have the ones that are the "rotten apples" of the group. One might be a thief or another one a racist, etc. To protect the family as a whole, the police union was formed. This seemed to work out fine until people started carrying phones with video cameras. That is when we were able to see how some members of the police departments were conducting themselves – bullying, beating, and murdering people they suspected of a crime. Because of these "bad apples" you have compromised integrity of the court system, judges and police officers as a whole. This is when I started to lose my trust of law enforcement; and when you lose trust, you lose respect for these institutions.

Back in the late 1960's and 1970's when the federal government started taking away a lot of social programs, like for mental health and kids' programs, all of a sudden, the police departments became "babysitters" for drunks, drug addicts and the homeless, and expected to be social workers and marriage counselors, too. Police are trained to deal with criminals, not with the social dramas of our society. They need to be trained on things like de-escalation techniques and ways to avoid using deadly weapons on people who are being stopped for questioning, etc. Police forces need to be re-trained in the difference between a criminal and an innocent citizen who may be a suspect.

Police departments need to restructure and reorganize, or whatever you want to call it, and acknowledge the fact that there is a racist element in their departments, and then take action to do something about it.

The police unions need some fixing, too. These are grown men whose job it is to know the difference between right and wrong. You can't think that allowing, or tolerating, violence-prone police officers is O.K. They need to understand that what happens when you compromise the integrity of police departments and the court systems is that you lose the trust and respect of the people – even for the officers who have good intentions and want to help people, regardless of their race.

It's time to end this. There is so much more to do. I have just skimmed over this history. There is so much more to learn. I can't tell you why I have written this paper – I just felt the need to explain to people who say "All Lives Matter" that they are right. So, when are African-American lives going to matter? When in U.S. history have African-American mattered? We need to do a better job of making the slogan "All Lives Matter" a reality.

Just like what is going on now with the Black Lives Movement. This is a needed movement and we need to look at history to see what has happened before the 1960's. You had the two political ideologies – working for social and economic equality of African-Americans. You had Malcolm X (1925 - 1965) and he was on the "Might Matters" right side of the two ideologies. He urged the African-American community to protect themselves against white aggression "by any means necessary" and that put him at odds with the non-violent teaching of Martin Luther King, Jr. (1929-1968). He was on "The Meek Shall Inherit the Earth" side of the two ideologies. As we can see back into history that these two political ideologies do not get a lot done. Working together to meet in the middle makes great things happen. This is the first time the white community has shown so much support, and this is very important. You don't want to lose it because of the old police trick of turning a protest into a riot. Make sure the media is there. They are good at telling us the causes of why it happens and so mostly we see the looting, the shootings and the violence – the stuff that sells and so the media and the political cartoonist do what they do best – fan the flames of hate and fear and racism and vandalism. That is what the viewer sees and they become afraid and you start to lose the support of the white community. It's the same trick the media and the police have been playing for hundreds of years.

Don't get caught up in the trap. The Black Lives Movement has won many battles, but you need to win the war on racism and BLM needs to take the American Flag and make it part of the protest because there is nothing more American than fighting for your rights for social and economic equality. Let's see what happens when the police attack protesters holding the American flag – our flag, not just the white supremacists' flag, as they claim; right now they are the only ones using it. Don't let them use the symbol of our rights as American citizens against us.

Conclusion

I hope you've learned some new things going down America's long dark road in these pages. I know I have. When you start getting into this subject, you soon realize that you're falling deep into a rabbit hole. Our racism problem is going to take years to resolve and for people to heal from it. I compiled this information to point out why Black Lives haven't really mattered in this country, so far – the truth of which is being revealed now more than ever. My hope is that what I have written may change some minds, or at least motivate some people to check out the huge amount of information on African-American history that is out there waiting to be discovered in books and online.

THE CARROTS ARE A VEGETABLE / BLACK LIVES MATTER
by Claire Saccardi

Carrots are a vegetable. It is a complete sentence, a statement, a fact.
That carrots are a vegetable changes nothing for the broccoli or the lettuce.
The broccoli is not less of a vegetable because the carrot is one also.
The lettuce's vegetable-ness is not diminished by the carrot being a vegetable, too.
As you read the proclamation of carrots as a vegetable, you probably didn't feel an urge to qualify the statement. You probably didn't feel other vegetables were threatened or needed to be defended. You probably didn't think anything else needed to be added to the sentence to make it a complete thought.

Black Lives Matters. It is a statement, a fact.
That a black life matters changes nothing for the life of a white woman, or a police officer.
The life of someone else does not matter less because a Black life matters, also.
Your own life's value is not diminished by a black life having value, too.
As you read the proclamation that Black Lives Matter, did you feel an urge to qualify it?
Did you feel threatened, or like you needed to defend something? Did you think something else needed to be added to the sentence to make it a complete thought?
If you did, take a moment and wonder why that is? Why is it easier to accept a statement about a vegetable than a statement about a Human Being?

RIOTS & MASSACRES

Many of the deaths that occurred in race-related riots between 1866 and 2009 were not reported or officially recorded. When statistics were available, I listed the number of people killed or wounded in each incident. A blank space in the "Killed/Wounded" column means that no death or wounded records could be found for that incident.

Date	Riot/Massacre	Killed / Injured
1824-1836	Providence, RI: Hard Scrabble and Snowtown riots	
1829	Cincinnati, OH	
1831	Virginia: Nat Turner's Slave Rebellion	
1834	New York City: Anti-Abolitionist Riot	
1835	Boston: The Gentlemen's Riots	
1835	Washington, D.C.: Snow Riots	
1836-41	Cincinnati, OH	
1838	Philadelphia, PA: Burning of Pennsylvania Hall	
1842	Philadelphia, PA: Lombard Street Riots	
1851	Christiana, PA	
1855	Memphis Riots	96 killed / 75 wounded
1863	Detroit, MI	
1866	New Orleans Riots	50 killed /150 wounded
1868	Pulaski Riots (KKK get noticed)	2 killed
1868	Opelousas, LA	200-250 killed
1868	Camilla, GA	12 killed / 30 wounded
1870	Eutaw, AL	9 killed / 54 wounded
1870	Lauren, SC	
1871	Meridian, MS	30 killed
1873	Colfax, LA Massacre	150+ killed
1874	Vicksburg, MS	300 killed

1874	New Orleans, LA	
1874	Coushatta, LA	20 killed
1875	Yazoo City, MS	5 killed
1876	**Homburg ?**	6 killed
1876	Ellenton, SC	30 killed
1898	Wilmington, NC	300 killed
1898	Lake City, SC	2 killed
1898	Greenwood, SC	12 killed / 100's wounded
1900	Robert Charles Riots ?	28 killed
1900	New York (city?)	
1906	Atlanta Riots	25 killed / 90 wounded
1906	Brownsville, TX	1 killed
1907	Onancock, VA	
1908	Springfield (state?) Riots	9 killed
1917	E. St. Louis, MO	250 killed
1917	Chester, PA	
1917	Philadelphia, PA	
1917	Houston, TX	5 killed
1919	**The Red Summer of 1919**	
	4/13 – Millen, GA	4 killed
	5/10 – Sylvester, GA	1 killed
	5/22 – Tampa, FL	
	5/22 – Houston, TX	
	5/29 – Putman, GA	
	5/31 – Monticello, MS	
	June – Atlanta, GA	
	6/6 – Boston, MA	
	6/11 – Tampa, FL	
	6/11-16 – Cincinnati, OH	
	6/13 – Memphis, TN	46 killed
	6/13 – New London, CN	
	6/25-6/28 – Omaha, NE	3 killed
	6/26-7/1 – Buffalo, NY	

6/27 – Macon, GA   1 killed
In July – Detroit
          Birmingham, AL
          Chicago, IL
          New Britain, CT
          Rochester, NY

The Red Summer of 1919 – continued

7/3 – Bisbee, AZ
7/5 – Scranton, PA   4 killed
7/6 – Dublin, GA
7/8 – Coatesville, PA
7/9 – Tuscaloosa, AL
7/7-31 – Philadelphia, PA
7/10 – Charleston, SC   6 killed
7/10 – Longview, TX   1 killed
7/12-17 – Newark, NJ
7/15 – Port Arthur, TX
7/16 – Plainfield, NJ
7/19-23 – Washington, D.C.   40 killed
7/21 – Norfolk, VA   2 killed
7/21 – Minneapolis, MN
7/22 – Detroit, MI
7/23 – New Orleans, LA   28 killed
7/24 – Cambridge, MD
7/26 – Hobson City, AL
7/27- 8/3 – Chicago, IL   23 killed / 537 wounded

7/28 – Newberry, SC
7/30 – Milwaukie, WI
8/4 – Hattiesburg, MS
8/5 – Lexington, NE   1 killed
8/6 – Texarkana, TX
8/18 – Mulberry, FL

	8/21 – New York, NY	40 killed
	8/27-29 – Ocmulgee, GA	1 killed
	Mid-Aug to Sept. – Baltimore, MD	
	8/27-28 – Laurensco, GA	1 killed
	8/30 – Knoxville, TN	30 killed
	10/1 – Elaine, AR	100-240 killed
	10/4-5 – Gary, IN	
	10/5 – Phillips County, AR	237 killed
	10/9 – Donora, PA	
	10/10 – Hubbard, OH	1 killed
	10/30 Corbin, KY	2 killed
	11/13 – Wilmington, DE	
	11/22 – Bogalusa, LA	1 killed
1921	Tulsa, OK	300 killed
1923	Rosewood, FL Massacre	30 killed
1935	Harlem Riots	3 killed
1943	Detroit Riots	34 killed
1943	Beaumont (St?)Riots	3 killed
1943	Harlem Riots	6 killed
1046	Columbia, TN	
1958	Battle of Hayes Pond, Maxton, NC	
1963	Cambridge, MD	
1964	Harlem Riots	1 killed
1964	Rochester, NY	
1964	Philadelphia, PA	
1965	Watts (L.A.) Riots	
1966	Hough Riots, Cleveland	
1966	North Omaha, NE	
1967	"The Long Hot Summer" or "The Summer of Love"	
1968	Orangeburg, SC Massacre	
1968	MLK assassination riots:	

	In Washington, DC, Chicago,
	Baltimore, Detroit, Trenton
	Pittsburg, Cincinnati,
	Wilmington, Louisville
1969	York, PA
1970	Jackson State MS Killings
1971	Camden, NJ
1972-	Escambia H.S. Riots
1977	in Pensacola, FL
1980	Miami, FL Riots
1980	Chattanooga, TN
1991	Crown Heights, Brooklyn, NY
1992	L.A. Riots
1996	St. Petersburg, FL Riots
2001	Cincinnati Riots
2003	Benton Harbor, MI Riots
2005	Toledo, OH Riots
2009	Oakland, CA Riots